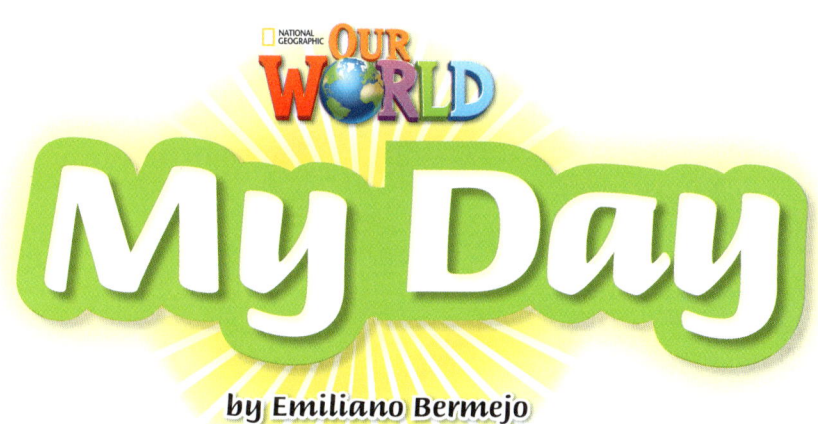

NATIONAL GEOGRAPHIC OUR WORLD

My Day

by Emiliano Bermejo

NATIONAL GEOGRAPHIC LEARNING | CENGAGE Learning

I get up every morning. I take a shower. Then I get dressed. Do you do that, too?

I don't get dressed, but I do take a shower. I make my own shower!

I eat breakfast every morning.
I like cereal for breakfast.
Do you like cereal, too?

I don't like cereal. I like bugs.
I eat bugs for breakfast!

Every afternoon, I play with my friends after school. Do you?

I don't go
to school,
but I do play
with my friends!

Every night, I eat dinner with my family.
Then I always do my homework.
After I do my homework, I relax with my family.
Do you?

I eat with my family at night,
but I don't do homework!
I relax with my family, too.

After I do my homework, I brush my teeth. Then I go to bed. Do you go to bed at night?

I never go to bed at night!
I am awake at night.
I sleep all day.

Facts About Animals

bald eagle

Daytime Animals

Some animals are awake during the day.
They eat and do other things in the daylight.
These animals are called **diurnal animals**.

honeybee

meerkat

orangutans

Nighttime Animals

Other animals are awake at night. They eat and move around in the dark. These animals are called **nocturnal animals**.

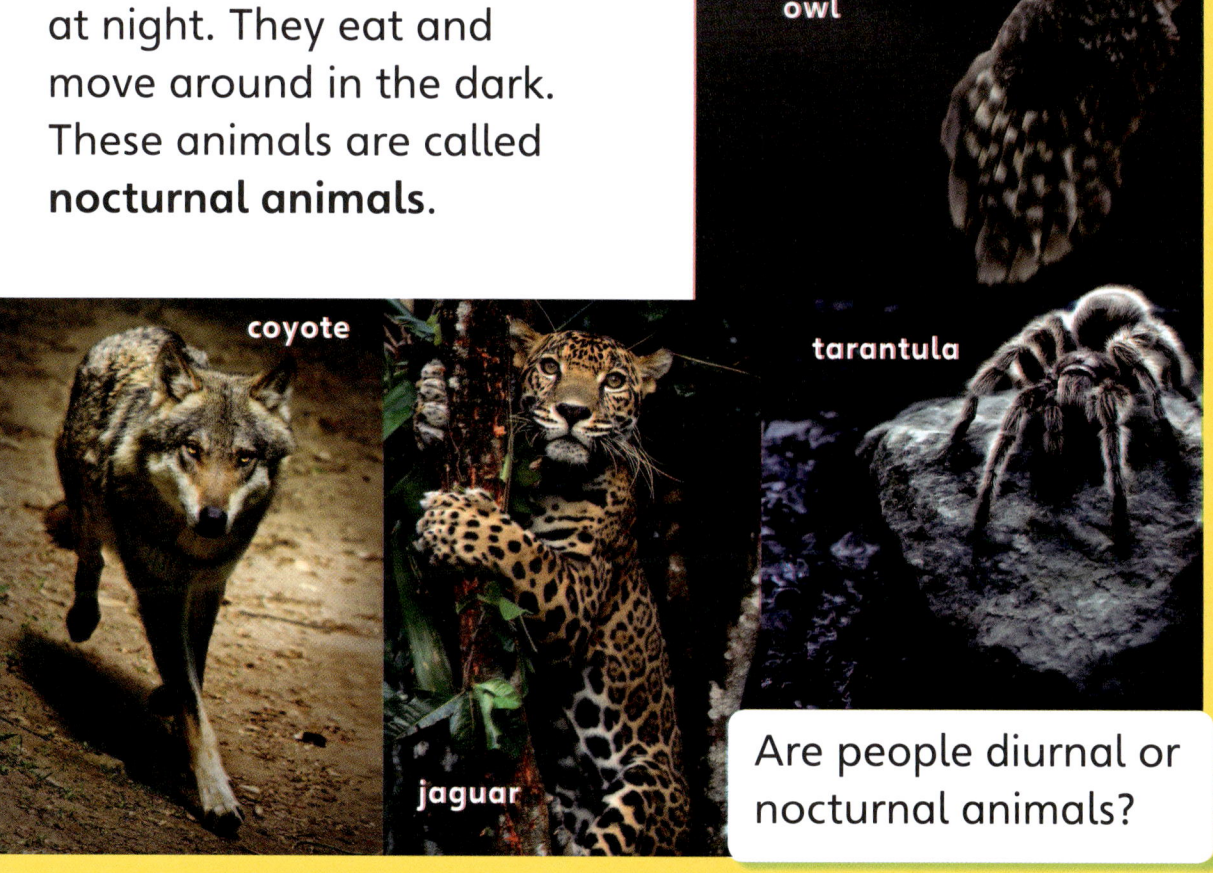

owl

coyote

jaguar

tarantula

Are people diurnal or nocturnal animals?

Fun with Daily Activities

What happens at each time of day? Write.

eat breakfast   **get up**   **eat dinner**   **go to school**   **go to bed**

6:45 A.M.

get up

7:00 A.M.

_____

8:00 A.M.

_____

6:00 P.M.

_____

8:00 P.M.

_____

When do you usually do these things? Circle the answer.

play with friends

(**afternoon**)   **night**

brush my teeth

morning   **afternoon**

do my homework

morning   **night**

get dressed

morning   **afternoon**

Glossary

awake

bugs

night

relax